OUTDOOR EXPLORERS

3 Southwest

Helen Foster James

Published in the United States of America
by Cherry Lake Publishing
Ann Arbor, Michigan
www.cherrylakepublishing.com

Reading Adviser: Marla Conn MS, Ed., Literacy specialist, Read-Ability, Inc.

Photo Credits: © IrinaK / Shutterstock.com, cover, 1; ©Monkey Business Images, 6; ©Tom Roche / Shutterstock.com, 8, 12; © Bakusova / Shutterstock.com, 10; © You Touch Pix of EuToch / Shutterstock.com, 10; © Tom Roche / Shutterstock.com, 11; © Kudrenko / Shutterstock.com, 11; © Andrew Orlemann / Shutterstock.com, 12; © vagabond54 / Shutterstock.com, 13; © Chris DeRidder and Hans VandenNieuwendijk / Shutterstock.com, 13; © Dennis W Donohue / Shutterstock.com, 14, 17; © Warren Metcalf / Shutterstock.com, 16; © dilynn / Shutterstock.com, 16; © Galina Gutarin / Shutterstock.com, 17; © Deep Desert Photography / Shutterstock.com, 18; ©chloe7992 / Shutterstock.com, 18; © Svetlana Foote / Shutterstock.com, 19; © lokvi / Shutterstock.com, 19; © In The Light Photography / Shutterstock.com, 20; © Asif Islam / Shutterstock.com, 20; © John D Sirlin / Shutterstock.com, 20; © Anton Foltin / Shutterstock.com, 20; © Anton Foltin / Shutterstock.com, 22; © Zhukova Valentyna / Shutterstock.com, 22; © Zack Frank / Shutterstock.com , 22; © Guy J. Sagi / Shutterstock.com, 22

Library of Congress Cataloging-in-Publication Data
Names: James, Helen Foster, 1951- author.
Title: Southwest / Helen Foster James.
Description: Ann Arbor : Cherry Lake Publishing, 2017. | Series: Outdoor explorers | Includes bibliographical references and index. | Audience: Grades K to 3.
Identifiers: LCCN 2016057053| ISBN 9781634728775 (hardcover) | ISBN 9781634729666 (pdf) | ISBN 9781534100558 (pbk.) | ISBN 9781534101449 (hosted ebook)
Subjects: LCSH: Natural history—Southwestern States—Juvenile literature.
Classification: LCC QH104.5.S6 J36 2017 | DDC 508.75—dc23
LC record available at https://lccn.loc.gov/2016057053

Cherry Lake Publishing would like to acknowledge the work of the Partnership for 21st Century Skills. Please visit www.p21.org for more information.

Printed in the United States of America
Corporate Graphics

Table of Contents

WASHINGTON

OREGON

IDAHO

NEVADA

CALIFORNIA

MONTANA

WYOMING

UTAH

NORTH DAKOTA

SOUTH DAKOTA

NEBRASKA

COLORADO

KANSAS

OKLAHO

ARIZONA

NEW MEXICO

TEXAS

ALASKA

HAWAII

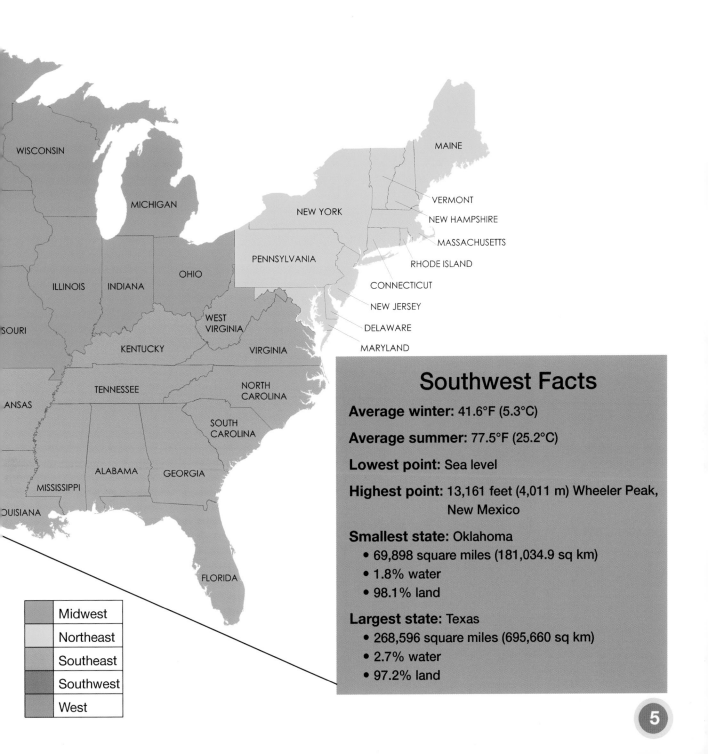

WISCONSIN

MICHIGAN

MAINE

NEW YORK

VERMONT

NEW HAMPSHIRE

ILLINOIS   INDIANA   OHIO

PENNSYLVANIA

MASSACHUSETTS

RHODE ISLAND

CONNECTICUT

SOURI

WEST
VIRGINIA

NEW JERSEY

DELAWARE

KENTUCKY

VIRGINIA

MARYLAND

ANSAS

TENNESSEE

NORTH
CAROLINA

SOUTH
CAROLINA

ALABAMA   GEORGIA

MISSISSIPPI

OUISIANA

FLORIDA

Southwest Facts

Average winter: 41.6°F (5.3°C)

Average summer: 77.5°F (25.2°C)

Lowest point: Sea level

Highest point: 13,161 feet (4,011 m) Wheeler Peak, New Mexico

Smallest state: Oklahoma
- 69,898 square miles (181,034.9 sq km)
- 1.8% water
- 98.1% land

Largest state: Texas
- 268,596 square miles (695,660 sq km)
- 2.7% water
- 97.2% land

Midwest

Northeast

Southeast

Southwest

West

It's time for a nature hike.
Let's see what we can see.

Not all saguaros grow an arm branch. But if they do, it can take up to 100 years for the arm to appear. How old do you think this cactus is?

Plants

I see a tall saguaro cactus in the desert. I find a shorter cactus. Pink flowers and white thorns are on it. I'm careful to look but not touch.

I see tumbleweeds. They blow all over the place. I try not to get in their way.

Desert Willow Tree

- Butterflies and hummingbirds are attracted to the nectar in the tree's flowers.

- They can be found in the desert by creeks and streams.

Hedgehog Cactus

- This common cactus is native to the Southwest.

- The flowers stay open at night.

Ocotillo

- The thin branches are covered in **prickly** thorns.

- After it rains, tiny leaves cover the sharp branches and orange flowers appear at the tips.

Parry's Agave

- This slow-growing plant can take 10 to 30 years before it has flowers.

- The flower **stalk** can reach a **height** of 20 feet (6 meters).

Pinyon Pine Tree

- New Mexico's official state tree since 1948.

- These slow-growing trees can live over 600 years.

Saguaro Cactus Blossom

- Arizona's official state flower since 1931.

- This cactus can grow up to 60 feet (18 m) tall, but it will take a very long time.

Texas Red Yucca

- Butterflies and hummingbirds can be found around this plant.

- The flower stalks can grow up to 5 feet (1.5 m) tall.

Tumbleweed

- A tumbleweed is a dried Russian thistle plant that broke away from the ground.

- Some tumbleweeds can be as big as a car!

The greater roadrunner is New Mexico's official state bird.
Why do you think the bird is named this?

Animals

There goes a roadrunner. It's running so fast. I see a Gila woodpecker make its home in a saguaro cactus. Where do other birds make their homes?

I see a small brown animal without fur curl into a ball. Its shell looks strong.

American Bison

- Oklahoma's official state animal since 1972.

- These large animals can weigh over 2,000 pounds (907 kilograms).

Gila Woodpecker

- The birds announce their presence with a high-pitched squeak.

- The male and female take turns sitting on their eggs.

Gopher

- These animals use their front teeth to dig tunnels underground.

- They use the pouches on the sides of their cheeks to carry things, like food.

Greater Roadrunner

- They eat almost anything, even rattlesnakes and their own young!

- These birds can run up to 20 miles (32 kilometers) per hour.

Jackrabbit

- These big-eared desert animals have strong back legs.

- Their diet includes seeds, leaves, grass, and cacti.

Javelina

- These desert animals live in groups of up to 50 javelinas.

- While they can't see well, they have a good sense of smell and hearing.

Nine-banded Armadillo

- Texas' official state small mammal since 1995.

- They can jump 3 to 4 feet (0.9 to 1.2 m) in the air.

Rattlesnake

- Arizona is home to 17 different types of rattlesnakes.

- These reptiles hiss and rattle their tails as a warning.

Spring

Summer

Fall

Winter

Weather

The spring air is warm. Sometimes the afternoons feel like summer.

The summer months are hot. The ground can feel like it's burning. I cool down in the shade.

It's **humid** during fall. I watch the clouds gather and grow dark. It might rain.

Winter nights and early mornings are cold. Sometimes it snows.

Desert

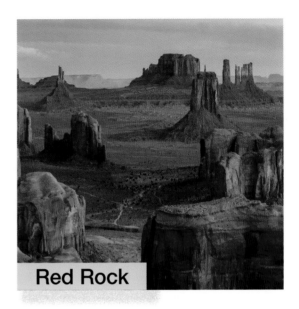

Red Rock

Mountain

Mesa

Geography

I hike in the desert. I see red rocks both big and small. I walk between the mountains.

I come across a hill with a flat top. What happened to its point?

I take a nature hike in my neighborhood. Many yards have wildflowers, short bushes, and rocks.

Where would you like to hike?

Find Out More

Cheshire, Gerard, and Peter Barrett (illustrator). *Mountains and Deserts*. New York: Crabtree, 2002.

Louv, Richard. *Last Child in the Woods: Saving Our Children from Nature-Deficit Disorder*. Chapel Hill: Algonquin Books, 2008.

Glossary

height (HITE) a measurement of how tall or high something is

humid (HYOO-mid) weather that is moist and usually very warm, in a way that is uncomfortable

mammal (MAM-uhl) a warm-blooded animal that has hair or fur and usually gives birth to live babies; female mammals produce milk to feed their young

native (NAY-tiv) an animal or a plant that lives or grows naturally in a certain place

nectar (NEK-tur) a sweet liquid from flowers

prickly (PRIK-uhl-ee) covered in prickles or thorns

reptiles (REP-tilez) cold-blooded animals with scaly, dry skin that crawl across the ground or creep on short legs

stalk (STAWK) the main stem of a plant from which the leaves and flowers grow

Index

About the Author

Helen Foster James is a volunteer interpretive naturalist for her local state park. She lives by the ocean and loves to hike in the mountains. She is the author of *S Is for S'mores: A Camping Alphabet* and more than 20 other books for children.